SELENA GOMEZ

POP STAR

KATIE LAJINESS

Big Buddy Books

An Imprint of Abdo Publishing
abdopublishing.com

BIG
BUDDY POP BIOGRAPHIES

abdopublishing.com

Published by Abdo Publishing, a division of ABDO, PO Box 398166, Minneapolis, Minnesota 55439.
Copyright © 2018 by Abdo Consulting Group, Inc. International copyrights reserved in all countries.
No part of this book may be reproduced in any form without written permission from the publisher.
Big Buddy Books™ is a trademark and logo of Abdo Publishing.

Printed in the United States of America, North Mankato, Minnesota.
092017
012018

THIS BOOK CONTAINS
RECYCLED MATERIALS

Cover Photo: Dimitrios Kambouris/Getty Images.
Interior Photos: Alberto E. Rodriguez/Getty Images (p. 11); Alexander Tamargo/Getty Images
(p. 15); Charley Gallay/Getty Images (p. 9); Christopher Polk/Getty Images (p. 17); Frederick M.
Brown/Getty Images (p. 5); Jason Merritt/Getty Images (p. 13); Kevin Winter/Getty Images
(pp. 6, 19, 21, 25); Mike Coppola/Getty Images (p. 27); Nicholas Hunt/Getty Images (p. 23);
Tommaso Boddi/Getty Images (p. 29).

Coordinating Series Editor: Tamara L. Britton
Contributing Editor: Jill Roesler
Graphic Design: Jenny Christensen

Publisher's Cataloging-in-Publication Data

Names: Lajiness, Katie, author.
Title: Selena Gomez / by Katie Lajiness.
Description: Minneapolis, Minnesota : Abdo Publishing, 2018. | Series: Big buddy pop biographies |
    Includes online resources and index.
Identifiers: LCCN 2017943935 | ISBN 9781532112140 (lib.bdg.) | ISBN 9781614799214 (ebook)
Subjects: LCSH: Gomez, Selena, 1992-.--Juvenile literature. | Singers--Juvenile literature. |
    Actors--Juvenile literature. | United States--Juvenile literature.
Classification: DDC 782.42164092 [B]--dc23
LC record available at https://lccn.loc.gov/2017943935

CONTENTS

BIG TALENT

Selena Gomez is a talented actress, singer, and businesswoman. For many years, she starred on the Disney Channel.

She has become one of today's most popular **entertainers**. Fans around the world love to see Selena on TV shows and magazine covers.

SNAPSHOT

NAME:
Selena Marie Gomez

BIRTHDAY:
July 22, 1992

BIRTHPLACE:
Grand Prairie, Texas

ALBUMS:
Stars Dance, Revival

FAMILY TIES

Selena Marie Gomez was born on July 22, 1992, in Grand Prairie, Texas. Her parents are Mandy Teefey and Ricardo Gomez. When Selena was five years old, her parents **divorced**. Selena has two younger half sisters.

In 2006 Selena's mom (*right*) married Brian Teefey (*left*).

DID YOU KNOW?
Selena was named after the Mexican-American singer Selena Quintanilla-Perez.

WHERE IN THE WORLD?

New Mexico

Oklahoma

Arkansas

Grand Prairie

Texas

Louisiana

MEXICO

GULF OF MEXICO

EARLY YEARS

From a young age, Selena was a natural **performer**. Her first TV **role** was on *Barney & Friends*. For two years, she danced and sang alongside a purple dinosaur named Barney.

When the show ended, Selena appeared in a few TV movies. At 12, she **auditioned** for the Disney Channel.

DID YOU KNOW?
Selena met fellow pop star Demi Lovato at the audition for *Barney & Friends*.

As a Disney Channel star, Selena often attended events for Disney shows.

DISNEY DARLING

Selena appeared on the Disney Channel for more than six years. Sometimes she played smaller **roles**.

In 2006, she was in an **episode** of *The Suite Life of Zack and Cody*. From 2007 to 2008, Selena played Mikayla on *Hannah Montana*. Later, she had a part in the show *The Suite Life on Deck*.

Selena attended the 2008 premiere of the *Tinker Bell* movie. This event was called the Pixie Premiere.

Selena was finally a leading lady. From 2007 to 2012, she was cast as the lead **role** in *Wizards of Waverly Place*. She played a witch named Alex Russo. Later, Selena starred in a movie based on the series.

DID YOU KNOW

In 2009, Selena joined friend Demi Lovato in the movie *Princess Protection Program*.

Years after *Barney & Friends*, Selena and Demi continued to be friends and attend events together.

RISING STAR

Already a famous actress, Selena decided to start a band. Selena Gomez & the Scene **released** three albums.

Selena also found success in larger **roles**. For the first time, Selena appeared on the big screen. Her first major film, *Ramona and Beezus,* earned $26 million!

Ramona and Beezus is based on a famous book series by Beverly Cleary. Selena plays a character named Beatrice. In the movie, she goes by the nickname Beezus.

SUPERSTAR

Fans couldn't get enough of Selena's *Revival* album. The singles "Same Old Love" and "Come and Get It" sold millions of copies in 2015 and 2016.

After her work with Disney ended, Selena continued to act. She grew her acting skills by playing both funny and serious **roles**.

DID YOU KNOW?
Selena played a superhero in Taylor Swift's music video, "Bad Blood."

Selena was a voice actor in *Hotel Transylvania* and the sequel. She plays Mavis, a vampire.

Life as a superstar keeps Selena busy. In 2016, she enjoyed her biggest **musical** success with her song "Same Old Love." The song remained on the *Billboard* Hot 100 chart for 28 weeks.

Selena has serious talent. But her fans still love to see her have fun. On *The Late Late Show with James Corden*, Selena and James sang her songs in a car.

Selena spent more than three months on her *Revival* Tour.

BIG COMEBACK

Growing up in the spotlight has been difficult for Selena. She struggled with fame and needed to get help. Selena went to **treatment** in 2014 while healing from an illness called lupus.

In 2017, Selena's illness grew worse. So, she had a kidney **transplant**. Since then, a healthy **lifestyle** has helped her heal from the **surgery**.

In interviews, Selena has said she sometimes feels lonely and sad on tour. Treatment helped Selena to feel better and continue her work.

BUSINESSWOMAN

Selena has been a smart businesswoman. She learned many new skills, such as clothing **design**. She used fun prints for her clothing line, Dream Out Loud.

Behind the camera, Selena started her own **production** company, July Moon. She has produced the movies *The Wizards Return: Alex vs. Alex* and *Rising*.

DID YOU KNOW?
Selena is studying Spanish. She hopes to record Spanish-language music.

Despite her busy schedule, Selena took time to accept a 2015 *Billboard* Women in Music Award.

AWARD SHOWS

As a popular **entertainer**, Selena has attended several **award** shows. She has been **nominated** for many awards. And, she has won some.

Over the years, Selena has won many Kids' and Teen Choice Awards. For these awards, the fans decide who wins.

At the 2016 American Music Awards, Selena gave an emotional speech. She thanked her fans for standing by her.

GIVING BACK

Selena has given her time and money to groups that help the arts, kids, and human rights.

Selena has worked with the United Nations Children's Fund since 2009. This group helps kids around the world stay healthy and safe.

In 2016, Selena attended a charity event at the Metropolitan Museum of Art in New York City, New York.

BUZZ

Today, Selena continues to act, sing, and work as a **producer**. Selena recently produced a Netflix series, *Thirteen Reasons Why*.

Selena's music career is still hot. She **released** a 2017 single with **musician** Kygo, "It Ain't Me." In 2018, Selena will continue her **role** as the voice of Mavis in *Hotel Transylvania 3*. Fans are excited to see what Selena does next!

Selena hosted the 2017 WE Day California event. Singer Alicia Keys joined her onstage.

GLOSSARY

audition (aw-DIH-shuhn) to give a trial performance showcasing personal talent as a musician, a singer, a dancer, or an actor.

award something that is given in recognition of good work or a good act.

design to make a pattern or sketch of.

divorce to legally end a marriage.

entertainer a person who performs for public entertainment.

episode one show in a series of shows.

lifestyle the usual way of life of a person, group, or society.

musical of or relating to music.

musician someone who writes, sings, or plays music.

nominate to name as a possible winner.

perform to do something in front of an audience. A performer is someone who performs.

producer a person who oversees the making of a movie, a play, an album, or a radio or television show. A production is a performance such as a play, a television show, or a movie.

release to make available to the public.

role a part an actor plays.

surgery (SUHRJ-ree) the treating of sickness or injury by cutting into and repairing body parts.

transplant the process or act of planting or moving elsewhere.

treatment medical or surgical care.

ONLINE RESOURCES

Booklinks
NONFICTION NETWORK
FREE! ONLINE NONFICTION RESOURCES

To learn more about Selena Gomez, visit **abdobooklinks.com**. These links are routinely monitored and updated to provide the most current information available.

 INDEX